Aurora

Elle Monus

Presentation by *BookLeaf Publishing*

Web: www.bookleafpub.com

E-mail: info@bookleafpub.com

ISBN: 9789357748889

First edition 2023

For Tyree, may my lessons and strengths be yours.

ACKNOWLEDGEMENT

I could write for days about how much I appreciate the people in my life that have made a difference or inspired me to be who I am today. Actually, getting them all in there is pretty daunting. So, I'm not.

If you have ever been in my life- know that I have learned from you and you have, in one way or another, shaped the woman I am today. And I really like her.

Thank you. This book is for you.

PREFACE

This book wasn't planned. In fact, I have a whole other book I've been sitting on for a couple of years now. But on Christmas Eve 2021 I sat in a too-small bathtub of what was now room-temperature water trying to figure out how I was going to change my life… again.

I found a Facebook Ad about a 21-day poetry challenge and decided it was time to learn how to write poetry. You know, just because I didn't know how.

Little did I know that being forced to come up with a poem every day for three weeks would actually help propel me in my self-healing journey. I laughed at my bad rhymes and silly prose; my heart ached, there were absolutely tears but also a warm and overwhelming feeling of forgiveness and self-love.

I found myself in these poems and while I'm no Emily Dickenson- I am Elle Monus.

Origin Story

Write a poem they said.
As if girls like me did.

Before stardust had a chance to settle
Before spirits rallied in the mud

Naked
Awakened
One life hasn't been taken.

Write a poem.
A girl like you must.

It glitters a path, of lightness and darkness.
Sitting in a fire, one moment is never enough.

Famed
Untamed
A new life has been spoken

I am the poem.
A poem of simplicity and lust.

Aurora

Spring came just in time
To wash out the last bit of dust

Everything is hers
If she just believes

Just believe,
Believe enough

They promised her silver
And they promised her gold

Find your way through
With the stories untold

There's mystery in her
Strength rising in each sunset

She is Aurora,
As her story unfolds

In life there is death
Frenzied, battered, and cold

Spring came just in time
Water pours out a new life

But they never told her
Her soul had already been sold.

The Burial

Drink her in
Her depths swallow you up
Only you know you'll never get enough.

Light comes tomorrow
But you'd never know tonight

Imagining she's never been touched
Everything now just feels so right.

Don't you love me, darling?
I've never loved once.

Spinning,
Laughing,
Feeling.

Drink her in
Each nerve on fire
Like the sun will never rise up

She's looking at you now
Is this good or bad luck?

Don’t you love me, darling?
I've never loved once.
But you, my love, will never get enough.

Be You

You're too this,
You're too that.

Not too skinny
But not too fat

Be her, be them
Wait patiently for midnight’s kiss

Step up to the table
But don’t you dare take that risk.

Be light,
Be bright

Be you; Be who?
I’m not sure that girl exists.

Brown skin
White skin

Do you want it natural,
Glowing or matte?

You're too this,
You're too that.

Not too curvy
But not too flat.

Be young,
Be fun

Be you; Be who?
That girl definitely does not exist.

Awakening

She pauses before she gets started
Knowing the answers, but not able to touch

This world means something
But “something” just isn’t enough

How those dreams must be guarded
Never wanting something so much.

She could stay here forever
But something new is calling her bluff

There is beauty in pain
A darkness that's warm

She could get there
if she wasn't so torn.

There is a rebirth on the horizon,
A rejuvenating light

Panic sets in
It’s never going to be just right

Power comes from the shadows
Laughter transforms from hurt

She’s ugly, flawed, and scared,
But there's magic in what she’s about to unearth.

Observance

Do not play with fire
My soul taught it how to dance
Quiet-feel its light

Mistakes

In a world where nothing is real
And nothing is right

She can't trust the others,
And she can't trust her mind

So many unknown answers
She’s searched for her whole life

Flowers kneel before her.
They cant trust her to be gentle

Petals wilted, stems withered
Each step is detrimental

She’s sunlight and rain
but something's not right

The warmth should give you life,
But her love doesn’t come without a fight

The Slow Change

Peace won’t come when you tell it so.
Dreams aren’t built until you really know.
Mirrors won’t tell what your presence shows.
Change only happens when you reap what you sow.
Fast stands still until you take it slow.
Dawn comes when you let it go.
Fail. Then you’ll really glow.

Float

It's a pretty strange thing, this life
One minute you know you won't make it
The next minute you think you might.

It's teeming with lessons
Your own untold story,
Unfolding and ready to write

People will see you
They'll point at the hate inside
And some of them will get it right

People will feel you
They'll grab onto the love inside
And try to take it with all their might

Do the best you can,
with nothing out of spite
Then grab onto my hand and hold on tight.

Balance

Even on your brightest days,
The darkness will always follow,
Welcoming you home.

Make peace with it.
The light will bring you your future,
The darkness is what makes you whole.

The Let Go

It's time to let you go now

I waited for you forever
Only to be touched for one night

I've danced with you, uneasy
Playing in your devilish light

Smiling and twirling, pulling closer
While looking into your eyes

I've never felt so at home here
It's peace, in love, and right

It's time to let you go now.

I waited for you forever,
My feet shake as they touch the ground

The dream of spending forever with you Is
broken
but I'm no longer bound

Unspoken words are hidden, painfully etched in time
With courage to speak them aloud now and ready to expound

It’s time to let you go now.

I love you. I love you,
More than any smell, sight, or sound

I hope one day we’ll meet again
And it's you that you have found.

You'll Learn

Sweet soul, you will lose.
You will lose so much in life that it hurts.

The blood of a thousand enemies won't quench
your thirst.
A million hands reach out, and each one you'll
refuse.

You'll feel empty, broken, and lost.
Anger and hate growing in the fighting that
ensues.

Darling, you will lose.
You will lose so much you won't be able to
count the cost.

You'll scream and you'll cry until you're numb
You'll spiral downward further than you ever
thought

No party, no success, no men will soothe you.
There's no peace, even in a hundred bottles of
booze.

My love, you will lose.
Getting back up is something only you can choose.

Dive

The broken swim in a void
Experiencing nothing and everything all at once

Lie to them carefully,
There's much to enjoy in their hunt

Don't let them see you healing,
They'll take you out with one swift punch

The deeper you go, the darker it gets,
Each truth is harder to confront

When they've been training their whole life for this,
Neither the corner nor the hat can contain the dunce

The Fall

As you slide down the wall, tears fall into your wine
You finally know now, that the world isn't on your time.

The floor is cold; your boxes are packed
You'll look around and realize- it was all an act.

Nobody loved you, not nearly enough
The callouses they left are ugly and rough.

The window calls you; you know what it wants
How dare you try to run there with a body so gaunt

Close your eyes, imagine your freedom
The darkness coaxes you- gently, in a deep hum

If you grew wings, you'd choose not to fly
You'll take one last look through tired, blurry eyes

Your world is over, you know that tonight.
There's nothing left in you, not even to fight.

Fall asleep my love, as darkness holds you tight
Your eyes won't open tomorrow, not even with
the morning light.

Renewal

The world is made for you
Before you know anything more than stardust
It glitters a path, dancing between darkness and light

The world is made of you
It breathes into you, heavy and robust
A tangled wonder with no beginning or end in sight

The world is made in you
Forged in fire, then covered in rust
Untouched, leaving the ruins in blight

The world is before you.
Take the long road if you must.
Just know that flowers will bloom, even at night.

Movement

Walk away.
Walk out.
Walk by.
Your dreams are waiting.

Hope

Passion suits you well
There is joy in each moment
Breathe- and enjoy it.

Now What?

It's real.
You deserve it; you deserve to feel

You did it.
All the work it takes to heal

It's not perfect.
But perfection isn't really real.

Feel it.
Its time to warm that heart of steel

Live.
The only thing better is going forward with zeal.

The Stump

I am the tree that gave too much.
Gave and gave and gave some more until I was only a stump.

But when I had nothing more to give, I had to learn how to live
And now my life is teaching others how not to jump.

Give a little; show a lot
Inspire and serve, but you're not everyone's rock.

Keep your trunk and all of your branches
In the end, the wind follows the tree that dances.

Good Morning, Aurora

Good morning Aurora,
How did you sleep?

Where are you going today,
With all that newfound relief?

I see you're looking up this morning
For the birds and the trees

You can do anything now
Did you, did you just believe?

Good morning Aurora,
How did you sleep?

What light are you shining today,
With all that unexplored peace?

I see you’re dancing this morning;
You seem so at ease

Good morning Aurora,
How did you sleep?

Who are you healing today,
With all that love running deep?

I see you've grown now,
Your fire has set you free.

Love, Momma

Look into my eyes just one last time
As the world falls away, so do I.
Everything I know here, I'll have to leave
behind
This vessel betrays me, but it was never mine

Oh Aurora, I only know love now, so don't you
cry
Even though, for you, this world has never been
kind
I hope its peace and love that you'll find
The light holds me now; it's time to say goodbye

www.ingramcontent.com/pod-product-compliance
Lightning Source LLC
LaVergne TN
LVHW020533160826
845677LV00015B/4038
* 9 7 8 9 3 5 7 7 4 8 8 8 9 *